STUDY GUIDE

Lessons from the Upper Room

Sinclair B. Ferguson

LIGONIER MINISTRIES

Renew your Mind.

LIGONIER.ORG | 800-435-4343

Introduction

What would it be like to spend five hours with Jesus the night before He was crucified? In the Farewell Discourses of John 13–17, our Lord spent close to that amount of time in a period that began with His washing the disciples' feet and ended with His High Priestly Prayer. In this series, Dr. Sinclair Ferguson explains these chapters in order to bring us into a greater knowledge of our Savior. Dr. Ferguson shows us the heart of Jesus and the hearts of His disciples during a time of anxiety but also approaching glory. In the process, we see clearly the need for the centrality of Christ in Christian life and worship.

1

Foot-washing in Five Stages

MESSAGE INTRODUCTION

The day before His crucifixion, Jesus shared His heart with His disciples. In what we know as the Upper Room or Farewell Discourse of John 13–17, He announced His betrayal and denial; foretold His death, glorification, and departure from this world; promised the coming Holy Spirit; and prayed in preparation for all that was to take place. In this series, Dr. Sinclair Ferguson walks us through these events, whose setting he calls "five wonderful hours with the Master." In this message, Dr. Ferguson especially examines Jesus' foot-washing in five stages, physically and theologically, in which He reveals Himself as the One who served us in order that we might serve others.

SCRIPTURE READINGS

John 13:1–12, Philippians 2:5–11

LEARNING OBJECTIVES

1. To understand the importance of the foot-washing incident in John 13
2. To recognize the theological significance behind this foot-washing
3. To realize that the centrality of Christ is foundational to the Christian life

QUOTATION

The doctrine, which points out to us the power and benefit of the coming of Christ, is far more clearly exhibited by [John] than by the rest. And as all of them had the same object in view, to point out Christ, the three former [gospels] exhibit his body, if we may be permitted to use the expression, but John exhibits his soul. On this account, I am accustomed to say that this Gospel is a key to open the door for understanding the rest; for whoever shall understand the power of Christ, as it is here strikingly portrayed, will afterwards read with advantage what the others relate about the Redeemer who was manifested.

—John Calvin

LECTURE OUTLINE

A. The Farewell Discourse occurs within the framework of the gospel of John.
    1. We view the discourse from two contexts.
        a. The gospel of John
        b. The contemporary world
    2. The gospel of John begins with a prologue regarding Jesus' incarnation and ends with an epilogue regarding Peter's restoration.
    3. Between these bookends, two volumes exist.
        a. *The Book of Signs* sets forth the work of Jesus (ch.1–12).
        b. *The Book of Passion* hides the glory of Jesus from all but His disciples (ch.13–21), within which the Farewell Discourse exists.
    4. Generally, John shows "the soul of Jesus," a description Calvin used for the gospel of John in contrast to the "body" presented in the other gospels.
    5. Specifically, the Farewell Discourse, as a time of intensive fellowship and teaching, might be called "five wonderful hours with the Master."

B. Jesus' washing of His disciples' feet occurs within the Farewell Discourse.
    1. Before the washing Satan tempted Judas to betray Jesus.
    2. Jesus arose from dinner as part of His mission to be a servant.
    3. Jesus disrobed as a servant to wash the feet of His disciples.
    4. Jesus exposed the pride of His disciples who refrained from washing others' feet.
    5. Peter failed to see beyond his dirty feet by resisting the washing.
    6. Jesus put His garments back on and returned to His place.

C. This dramatic parable points to the five "foot-washing" stages of Philippians 2.
    1. *Jesus descended from the highest origin* (2:6), with a mission of washing feet as He set forth His identity and work (John 13:1).
    2. *Jesus underwent profound humiliation* (2:6–7), disrobing to wash proud humans' feet (John 13:4–5).
    3. *Jesus suffered death on the cross* (2:8), washing the dirty feet of His disciples (John 13:6–8,12).
    4. *Jesus experienced glorious exaltation* (2:9), taking up His clothes again to return to His place (John 13:12).
    5. *Jesus sits enthroned in heaven above every name* (2:10–11), wanting His disciples to "understand" the need to kneel (John 13:7, 12).

STUDY QUESTIONS

    1. The Farewell Discourse occurs within John's Book of Signs, which sets forth the person and work of Jesus.
        a. True
        b. False

2. We come to the Farewell Discourse from two contexts:
   a. That of the gospel of John and Philippians 2
   b. That of the Book of Signs and the Book of Glory
   c. That of the gospel of John and the Synoptic Gospels
   d. That of the gospel of John and the contemporary hearer

3. Peter initially protested that Jesus should not wash him and, in so doing, failed to see beyond his dirty feet.
   a. True
   b. False

4. Jesus washed the feet of His disciples before Satan tempted Judas to betray Jesus.
   a. True
   b. False

5. John Calvin's description that the gospel of John reveals the soul of Jesus is held:
   a. In connection with His possession of a body
   b. In contrast to His possession of a body
   c. In connection with His coming as the God-man
   d. In contrast to the other gospels emphasizing His body

6. The foot-washing performed by Jesus comes as a dramatic _____ of His identity and work.
   a. Parable
   b. Narrative
   c. Idiom
   d. Hyperbole

7. Jesus washed His disciples' feet in order to:
   a. Comfort them in their grief
   b. Expose their pride and self-investment
   c. Institute a perpetual ordinance for the church
   d. Prepare the disciples for dinner

8. Christ's washing His disciples' feet manifested:
   a. His humility
   b. His exaltation
   c. His redemptive work
   d. All of the above
   e. None of the above

BIBLE STUDY

1. Recognizing the importance of parallel accounts for the Last Supper in the other gospels, how does Luke 22:24–30 heighten the significance of the foot-washing?

2. As we read our Bibles, it does not take long to realize how the historical setting contributes significantly to our understanding of a passage. How do we benefit by knowing that washing guests' dirty feet (soiled by travels on dirt paths and roads) was a menial task typically assigned to household servants?

3. What is the connection between John 10:17–18 and Jesus' disrobing, then taking up His clothes again in order to return to His place at the table?

DISCUSSION QUESTIONS

1. Dr. Ferguson calls attention to John Calvin's description of the gospel of John as setting forth the "soul" of Jesus in a more pronounced way than the Synoptic Gospels, which focus more on the "body" of Jesus. Discuss the meaning of this claim. Why must we be careful to qualify Calvin's argument?

2. Dr. Ferguson notes that in the Farewell Discourse, "one of the things we will discover personally is that our whole framework of reference is moved to have Jesus Christ at its center." Explain what Dr. Ferguson means by this as it relates to Christ and to us.

3. What does Dr. Ferguson mean when he claims that this foot-washing symbolized not just our justification but also our delivery from the Satanic powers that bind us?

APPLICATION

1. You cannot truly serve others without the humbled and exalted Savior serving you. Do you understand what He has done? Have you personally experienced His washing?

2. Those who are washed or served by the kneeling and exalted Christ will be transformed to serve others even in the most menial tasks. Come up with at least one concrete way that you can do this.

3. Christians continue to struggle with thoughts of greatness, which blinds us to the needs of others. Think of one specific example of how this occurs in families and another example of how it occurs in the church.

FOR FURTHER STUDY

D.A. Carson, *The Gospel According to John*
Leon Morris, *The Gospel According to John*
R.C. Sproul, *John*

2

Do for Others What
Has Been Done for You

MESSAGE INTRODUCTION

Most people are familiar with the "Golden Rule" of Matthew 7:12: "Do to others as you would have them do to you." In this message, Dr. Ferguson connects this well-known maxim to the foot-washing in John 13. As he continues to open up this event, Dr. Ferguson discusses the gospel as the key to understanding what Christ has done in washing His disciples' feet and what He wants them to do in washing the feet of others. Dr. Ferguson challenges Christians to "do for others what has been done for you" by Christ.

SCRIPTURE READINGS

John 13:12–20; Matthew 7:12

LEARNING OBJECTIVES

1. To properly apply the command to "wash feet" in Christ
2. To find a foundation for serving others in the gospel of Christ
3. To understand the importance of our call as servants and messengers of Christ

QUOTATION

What was the mystery of this his washing their feet? It was, as to give them an example of mutual love and humility, so to signify his washing away their sins; thus, verses 8 and 10, himself interprets it. It is true indeed, that, now he is in heaven, he cannot come to wash the feet of their bodies, but he would signify thus much thereby, that those sinners that will come to him when in his glory, he will wash away all their sins. "He loved his church, and gave himself for it, that he might sanctify and cleanse it with the washing of water, that he might present it to himself a glorious church, not having spot or wrinkle," etc. (Eph. 5:25–27).

—Thomas Goodwin

LECTURE OUTLINE

A. We see Jesus from different perspectives in the foot-washing of John 13.

    1. In this message, our goal is to move from understanding the foot-washing to experiencing the blessing of it.

    2. In a popular optical illusion, we view in the same picture both an old hag and a beautiful young woman, as though a transformation takes place before our eyes.

    3. In a similar manner, we see different views of the same Jesus in the foot-washing.

        a. Our Savior who brings the blessing of salvation

        b. Our example who provides the blessing of a transformed life

B. We find the foundation for foot-washing in the gospel.

    1. The gospel remains the key for the disciples to "understand" now (v. 12) what they could not earlier (v. 7).

    2. The gospel energizes the way we live by transforming the way we think (vv. 14–15; see also Rom 12:1–2).

        a. The Christian life does not lie primarily in our emotions.

        b. The Christian life lies primarily in our understanding of the gospel.

    3. The gospel provides the core for the Christian life (v. 15) carried out according to the Golden Rule (Matt. 7:12).

        a. We first recall what Jesus has done for us.

        b. We then carry out the same for others.

C. We approach the key elements of foot-washing in Christ.

    1. *What Jesus has done*: He clothed himself with humility that we might do the same.

    2. *Who Jesus is:* He is the eternal Son and Lord of Glory who laid the foundation for the Christian life in His person and work.

    3. *Who we are*: We are those washed by Jesus to become:

        a. Bondservants of our Master with our will as His own serving others

        b. Messengers with a sweet-smelling aroma who represent our glorious Redeemer

STUDY QUESTIONS

    1. The optical illusion of the old hag turning into a beautiful young woman helps us see Jesus as our Savior and example from different perspectives.

        a. True

        b. False

    2. Jesus assumed that His disciples could understand what He was doing with the foot-washing in John 13:7, only to change His mind later (v.12).

        a. True

        b. False

3. According to Dr. Ferguson, the gospel "transforms the way we think" but it cannot give "energy to the way in which we speak and live."
    a. True
    b. False

4. The foundation for the Christian life lies primarily in:
    a. Our emotions
    b. Our instincts
    c. Understanding the gospel
    d. Asking the question, "What would Jesus do?"

5. The principle of Romans 12:2:
    a. Originated in the writings of Paul
    b. Sees a transformed mind as foundational for a changed life
    c. Does not take away from the fact that the Christian life starts with what we "feel" in our heart
    d. Emphasizes the power of the human mind

6. Getting to the key elements of foot-washing involves asking:
    a. What has Jesus done?
    b. Who is Jesus?
    c. Who are we?
    d. All of the above
    e. None of the above

7. Seeing the same Jesus from two points of view in the foot-washing concerns viewing Him as:
    a. Our Redeemer who brings the blessing of salvation
    b. Our Example who provides the blessing of a transformed life
    c. Our Captain who leads us to victory in our resurrected life
    d. Both a and b
    e. Both b and c

BIBLE STUDY

1. Dr. Ferguson uses the illustration of handwriting from his childhood and its association with the idea of "following" (as a pattern) the steps of Christ in 1 Peter 2:21. Examine this word in its context in 1 Peter 2. What is the connection between this passage and the Golden Rule (Matt. 7:12) mentioned in this message (for example, "Do for others what has been done for you")?

2. This message calls attention to Peter's exhortation in 1 Peter 5:5 that Christians "clothe" themselves with humility. Examine this challenge in its context in 1 Peter 5. How does this verse relate to the humility and exaltation of Christ and His centrality in the Christian life? Discuss how this verse and 1 Peter 2:21 connect to John 13.

3. This message makes note of Paul's exhortation in Romans 12:2 to be "transformed" by the renewing of our minds. Examine this passage in its context in Romans 12. From Romans 12, is this transformation a once-and-done deal, or is it an ongoing process? What is the connection of verse 2 to verse 1? From the discussion on conformity to the world in verse 2, what happens when this renewal of the mind suffers neglect in the Christian life?

DISCUSSION QUESTIONS

1. Perhaps you have at some point heard the question, "Must we live according to the Golden Rule?" In this message, Dr. Ferguson seems to answer, "Yes and no." Why would he respond this way?

2. With at least a loose connection to Charles Sheldon's *In His Steps* (1896), modern Christianity has made the expression WWJD ("What would Jesus do?") very popular. Interestingly, this book was an early expression of liberal Christianity emphasizing Jesus as a supreme example to the neglect of His substitutionary atonement. This fact, in connection with our current message, shows us that WWJD can be harmful if not preceded by WHJD: "What has Jesus done?" Why is this the case?

3. Some churches practice ceremonial foot-washing because they believe it is required to obey Jesus' teaching that His disciples should do what He has done for them. How are these churches both right and wrong in their response? How does the context of the foot-washing in John 13 (mentioned in the first message) help us here?

APPLICATION

1. We often hear preaching about what we need to avoid in order to keep the world from squeezing us into its mold. Our current message makes clear that we must not only turn from such conformity but also be transformed by the renewing of our minds. Think of two concrete ways that "renewing" your mind according to the gospel can be cultivated (for example, in a world driven by self-righteous anger, I can memorize and meditate regularly upon Galatians 6:1 when dealing with the sin of others).

2. Dr. Ferguson shares the convicting lesson he learned while watching a waitress drop a stack of dishes. He was illustrating the tendency of Christians to withhold help from those we believe are below us. Can you think of a specific example at home, school, church, or work when you failed to do something for someone in need, simply because you thought them not worthy of your help? Pray that you would never fail to assist someone you are able to assist.

3. Dr. Ferguson also shares the claim that the Scots smell of milk to illustrate the aroma we give off for Christ—the way we affect the spiritual atmosphere around us—as His representatives. How do you affect the spiritual atmosphere around you? Do you find that you attract people to Christ? Why or why not?

FOR FURTHER STUDY

Thomas Goodwin, *The Heart of Christ in Heaven toward Sinners on Earth*, in *Works*, vol. 4

Jonathan Edwards, "Christ the Example of Ministers," in *Altogether Lovely: Jonathan Edwards on the Glory and Excellency of Jesus Christ*

3

A Glimpse into the Heart of the Master

MESSAGE INTRODUCTION

Even though we know that Jesus never sinned, we have a difficult time coming to grips with the fact that He could become agitated. Still, knowing that He would be betrayed and who would carry out the task, He was indeed deeply troubled, but hardly surprised. He knew His destiny, and He, not Judas or anyone else, governed it. In this lesson, Dr. Ferguson reveals the mind and heart of our Savior who was intimately familiar with all of the painful experiences of humanity. In an atmosphere polluted by the presence of His betrayer, we are reminded again that the suffering of Jesus was not a pathway to defeat but an entrance to victory.

SCRIPTURE READINGS

John 13:21–31; Psalm 41:9

LEARNING OBJECTIVES

1. To discover the heart of Christ in His humanity by way of the painful betrayal He would endure
2. To recognize the signs of those who betray Jesus, specifically Judas
3. To realize that Jesus alone maintained control of His destiny for the cross

QUOTATION

Let us mark, lastly, in these verses, the extreme hardness which comes over the heart of a backsliding professor of religion. This is a thing which is most painfully brought out in the case of Judas Iscariot. One might have thought that the sight of our Lord's trouble, and the solemn warning, "One of you shall betray Me," would have stirred the conscience of this unhappy man. But it did not do so. . . . Like one whose conscience was dead, buried, and gone, he rises and goes out to do his wicked work, and parts with his Lord forever.

—J.C. Ryle

LECTURE OUTLINE

A. Jesus confesses that He is deeply troubled.
   1. The Salvador Dali painting "Christ of Saint John of the Cross" depicts a flying crucifix with a Savior who never touches the earth, as Francis Schaeffer notes.
   2. In contrast, John in his gospel presents a Jesus firmly anchored to this world (John 1:14).
   3. Thus, Jesus entered not just the reality but also the frailty of human existence.
   4. Part of this experience involved Jesus' agitation of spirit here (see also John 12:27).
      a. In contrast to His challenge not to be troubled (John 14:1)
      b. Because His betrayer was present with Him
      c. To relieve those who experience the same (Heb. 2:18)

B. Jesus reveals the identity of His betrayer.
   1. Unlike current readers of John's gospel, none of the disciples except Judas knew he would betray Jesus.
      a. Even though he witnessed the miracles of Jesus
      b. Even though he professed to be a disciple of Jesus
   2. As the gospel unfolds, John prompts the reader to keep an eye on Judas, the betrayer of Jesus (e.g. John 6:71; 12:4–6).
      a. One who faked concern for the poor
      b. One who pilfered money as the treasurer
   3. How did Jesus know that Judas would betray Him?
      a. Not simply because Jesus was God
      b. Because the Scriptures revealed it (Ps. 41:9; see also Gen. 3:15)
      c. Because Jesus possessed perfect insight
   4. Judas manifested marks of his betrayal, like other professed followers of Christ.
      a. Being repelled by Jesus' displays of grace
      b. Disguising rather than confessing sin unmasked by Jesus
      c. Seeing Jesus as our servant rather than our Master

C. Jesus settles His own destiny.
   1. Jesus suffered as a victim at the hands of Judas, the soldiers, and religious and secular authorities.
   2. None of these abusers settled His destiny, for He alone could do so.
   3. The end begins with Jesus dismissing Judas to carry out his betrayal.
   4. Still, the treachery set in motion shows that Jesus was in control of events.
      a. Under the sovereign control of the Father
      b. For the glory of Jesus
      c. For the salvation of the world

5. As Luther asserted, "The devil is God's devil," and when he strikes Jesus' heel, his own head gets crushed.

STUDY QUESTIONS

1. The Salvador Dali painting "Christ of St. John of the Cross" presents a freely floating Jesus without any real connection to this world.
    a. True
    b. False

2. Jesus did not wash the feet of Judas because the former knew the latter had nothing to do with Him as His betrayer.
    a. True
    b. False

3. The betrayer of Jesus was known by Jesus and Judas but unknown at this time by the other disciples.
    a. True
    b. False

4. Jesus was troubled in spirit because:
    a. His disciples were heartbroken about His departure.
    b. His betrayer was present in the room.
    c. He would die on the cross.
    d. His disciples did not grasp the reason for washing their feet.

5. "The devil is God's devil," said _____ .
    a. Augustine
    b. Dante
    c. Luther
    d. Bunyan

6. Ultimately, _____ was responsible for the destiny of Jesus, the One who would soon be crucified.
    a. Caiphas
    b. Pontius Pilate
    c. Judas
    d. Satan
    e. None of the above

7. The following are true of Judas:
   a. He denied being a follower of Jesus.
   b. Jesus did not wash his feet.
   c. He stole money to help the poor.
   d. All of the above
   e. None of the above

8. Jesus knew that Judas would betray Him because:
   a. He was God.
   b. He knew from the Bible that someone would.
   c. He possessed perfect discernment.
   d. All of the above
   e. None of the above

BIBLE STUDY

1. Examine Psalm 41:9, which predicts the betrayal of Jesus. As you consider this verse, do you think that Jesus knew from the start that Judas was the one who would betray Him? Answer this in connection to what Dr. Ferguson says about Jesus' perfect human insight and in light of John 2:25 and Philippians 2:6–8. Finally, what is the link between the "lifting" of the heel in Psalm 41:9 and Genesis 3:15?

2. Mark 10:45 states that Jesus "came not to be served but to serve, and to give his life as a ransom for many." How does this truth fit with the foot-washing episode and the idea that the mark of a betrayer is to treat Jesus as our servant rather than Master?

3. Examine Psalm 118:22–24. How does this passage relate to the idea that Jesus settled His own destiny, not Judas? How do people often take verse 24 out of context?

DISCUSSION QUESTIONS

1. Salvador Dali claimed to get a vision for his painting mentioned above through a "cosmic" dream depicting Christ as the very "unity of the universe." In light of this message, what do you make of Dali's claim for this depiction?

2. One of the marks of someone who betrays Jesus is that he or she treats Jesus as a servant rather than bowing to Him as Master. The preachers of the prosperity gospel do this in a blatant manner. How might we do this in a subtle way?

3. In discussing that Jesus settled His own destiny, not Judas, Dr. Ferguson mentions Luther's claim that "the devil is God's devil." What does Luther mean by this? Some evangelicals would find this idea problematic. Why do you think this is the case? How would you answer them?

APPLICATION

1. John warns us of the Judas to come well before he actually betrays Jesus. We do not get such clear forewarnings about someone who professes but ends up denying Christ. Still, we must beware of a growing spirit of Judas that tramples Christ underfoot and insults the Spirit of grace (Heb. 10:29). Take time to pray specifically that God will keep such a tendency from developing in you, your family, and your church.

2. Forget about the prosperity gospel preachers for a moment. Think of one way in which you tend to make Jesus your servant rather than serving Him. Prayerfully consider how you can correct such a tendency.

3. We must take care to accept full responsibility for our sin without blaming God or the devil. Think about it. Have you at times attributed too much to the forces of evil or providential trials for your own moral failures? Meditate on 1 Corinthians 10:13 for encouragement when you face temptation.

FOR FURTHER STUDY

Thomas Boston, *Amiable Professors Falling Short of Heaven*
A.W. Pink, *The Sovereignty of God*
Thomas Watson, *A Body of Divinity*

4

Glorified Yet Denied

MESSAGE INTRODUCTION

The polluted atmosphere changed with the departure of Judas from the Upper Room. Jesus then more freely opened Himself and His plan to the remaining disciples. The moment anticipated in John 1:14 had come. The Son of Man had arrived at His glory and the kingdom would be expanded as a result. Yet, as Dr. Ferguson shows in this lesson, the way down to the cross was the way up to glory. He also makes clear that the crucifixion is not just a time of pity or sadness, but also a time of triumph. The disciples did not understand, and Peter's own ignorance would lead to his denial of the glorified Savior. In this way, John 13 comes to an end with a glimpse of both glory and failure.

SCRIPTURE READINGS

John 13:31–38; Daniel 7:9–14

LEARNING OBJECTIVES

1. To recognize that the crucifixion of Jesus was the way to His glory
2. To understand that the title *Son of Man* must be applied to the exaltation and not just to the humiliation of Jesus
3. To grasp the dynamics behind Peter's denial and how it relates to our own lives

QUOTATION

Peter denied his master, once, twice, thrice, and that with open oath; yet Christ receives him again without any the least hesitation or stick. Yea, he slips, stumbles, falls again, in downright dissimulation, and that to the hurt and fall of many others; but neither of this doth Christ make a bar to his salvation, but receives him again at his return. . . . Now all these are examples, particular instances of Christ's readiness to receive the backsliders to mercy; and, observe it, examples and proofs that he hath done so are, to our unbelieving hearts, stronger encouragements than bare promises that so he will do.

—John Bunyan

LECTURE OUTLINE

A. Jesus announces His glory as the Son of Man.

    1. As most realize, this title refers to the humanity of Jesus.

    2. As many do not recognize, this title also denotes the exaltation of Jesus.

    3. Jesus draws on the picture of the Son of Man observed in Daniel 7.

        a. He ascends victoriously to His throne.

        b. He shares His triumph with the saints of the Most High.

    4. Jesus sees this time to be "glorified" as the time to be exalted at His Father's right hand.

    5. "The way up to the throne of God is the way down to the humiliation of the cross."

    6. The Son of Man achieves glory by crucifixion, because He did nothing worthy of death.

        a. Condemned to death but declared to be innocent

        b. Labeled "King of the Jews" by Pilate

        c. Victimized but without expecting pity

B. Jesus predicts His denial at the hands of a disciple.

    1. Jesus moves from talk of departing for glory to a call for mutual love.

    2. Peter loved the idea of a victorious Messiah but not a crucified Messiah.

        a. He failed to realize that a disciple follows a crucified Savior.

        b. He failed to see that triumph comes through suffering.

        c. He failed to recognize his flimsy claim of love unto death.

    3. Jesus foretells Peter's denial that arises out of his ignorance.

    4. Peter's clueless spirit calls us back to his earlier protest.

        a. He resisted the foot-washing.

        b. He rejected the idea of what the washing meant.

    5. Peter did eventually come to understand (see 1 Pet. 3:18).

        a. Jesus died for sinners.

        b. The just died for the unjust.

    6. Peter did eventually experience restoration.

        a. He reminds us that failure in the Christian life need not be final.

        b. He leaves us with an example for usefulness and fruitfulness.

STUDY QUESTIONS

    1. The title *Son of Man* refers to the humanity of Jesus.

        a. True

        b. False

    2. The title *Son of Man* does not refer to the exaltation of Jesus.

        a. True

        b. False

3. The way up to the throne of God is the way down to the humiliation of the cross.
    a. True
    b. False

4. Jesus draws on the picture of the Son of Man in _____ to announce His glory in John 13.
    a. Isaiah 53
    b. Ezekiel 37
    c. Psalm 22
    d. Daniel 7

5. Peter's denial of Jesus arises out of his _____ regarding Jesus' achievement of glory.
    a. Ignorance
    b. Knowledge
    c. Refusal
    d. Hesitancy

6. That Jesus achieved glory by death since He did nothing worthy of death is shown by:
    a. His condemnation by those who declared Him innocent
    b. His title *King of the Jews* by Pilate
    c. His victimization without expectation of pity
    d. Both a and b
    e. All of the above

7. The Old Testament picture that Jesus uses to announce His glory as the Son of Man involves:
    a. Descending to the realm of Hades
    b. Ascending to a victorious throne
    c. Sharing a triumph with the saints
    d. Both a and b
    e. Both b and c

8. Peter's denial of Jesus is connected to his earlier protest during the foot-washing when:
    a. He refused to have his feet washed
    b. He rejected the idea of what the washing meant
    c. He wanted his hands and head washed too
    d. Both a and b
    e. Both b and c

BIBLE STUDY

1. Read John 1:14. Dr. Ferguson says this verse (see also 2:11; 7:39; 11:4, 40) anticipates the moment of the pronouncement of glorification when Judas leaves the room. Clearly, glory is attached to the crucifixion, which we usually see as part of the humiliation of Christ. What does this suggest about the connection between the cross and glory?

2. Study Daniel 7:9–14 in connection with John 13:31. Given that the title *Son of Man* can refer to humanity in general (e.g. Ps. 8:4; Ezek. 2:1) and is attributed to Christ in His humiliation, what is striking about Daniel 7 (in relation to the mention of the Ancient of Days, a general expression of God in His deity) and what takes place with the Son of Man?

3. What do John 19:19–22 and Pilate's inscription have to do with glory through the cross? Do not miss the protest to and response from Pilate, called by some an unwitting prophet, as well as the reference to "Nazareth."

DISCUSSION QUESTIONS

1. John Geree said of the Puritan man, "His own life he accounted a warfare, wherein Christ was his captain, his arms, prayers, and tears. The Cross his banner, and his motto, *Vincit qui patitur*." This Latin phrase means, "He who endures, conquers." How should this "motto" inform the church today?

2. Dr. Ferguson insists that looking on the crucifixion as simply a time of "intense sadness" misses the point. Hebrews 12:2 tells us that Jesus endured the cross and treated its shame as nothing because of the joy of exaltation before Him and all that came with it. With this in mind, how should we respond to books and movies that portray the cross as only full of grief?

3. The Puritans cautioned that the difference between backsliding and apostasy is not immediately apparent. Consider the denial of Peter in connection with the betrayal of Judas. How are the two alike? How are they different? How does this reality instruct the church and its officers to be careful in making judgments about "wheat and tares"?

APPLICATION

1. It is easy for us, like Peter, to want to know the power of Christ's resurrection without a desire to share in His sufferings (Phil. 3:10). Why do we have this tendency and what can we do about it?

2. Dr. Ferguson mentions a hypothetical poll for our favorite disciple. He rightly points out how much most of us identify with Peter, who had "failure" written all

over his ministry. With the Bunyan quote above in mind, think about how much our failings can deflate us and how easily we can look down upon others in their "stumbles." Meditate upon the fact that failure in the Christian life need not be final, for Christ freely offers restoration to believers who deny Him but then repent. Give thought to how you can apply this truth to your life and others' lives.

3. Think of a time when you denied Christ in word or deed. Have you repented of it? Pray that God would strengthen you to stand for Christ in every situation.

FOR FURTHER STUDY

Augustine, *Lectures on the Gospel of John*, vol. 2, tract 66
Sinclair B. Ferguson, *In Christ Alone: Living the Gospel Centered Life*
R.C. Sproul, *The Glory of Christ*

5

Troubled That
You May Not Be

MESSAGE INTRODUCTION

You may not realize this, but the verse best known in the gospel of John is probably John 14:1— not John 3:16. At funerals we often hear, "Let not your hearts be troubled," with the hope of giving comfort to grieving hearts. As Dr. Ferguson notes, this verse is often taken out of context, as people fail to understand the foundation for the consolation that Christ offers. Ironically, it arises out of the very gospel-centered suffering that our Savior endured on behalf of sinners. In this lesson, then, we find counsel for troubled hearts in general and to pessimistic Thomas and self-sufficient Philip in particular. In the end, Jesus was troubled in order that His disciples may not be.

SCRIPTURE READINGS

John 14:1–15; John 1:14, 17

LEARNING OBJECTIVES

1. To understand that Jesus was troubled for us in His humiliation that we may find comfort in our own troubles
2. To recognize Jesus as the exclusive way to the Father
3. To realize that Jesus identifies with His Father in everything

QUOTATION

Yea, believers themselves would live within the sight of this, and not forget their frailty; for though there be a change wrought in them, yet they are not perfect, but will have need of Christ as the way, the truth, and the life, till he bring them in, and set them down upon the throne, and crown them with the crown of life. And, O happy they, who must not walk on foot without this guide leading them by the hand, or rather carrying them in his arms. Let all them who would make use of Christ remember what they were, and

22

what they are, and keep the sense of their frailty and misery fresh; that seeing their need of him, they may be in better case to look out to him for help and supply, and be more distinct in their application of him.

—John Brown of Wamphray

LECTURE OUTLINE

A. Jesus provides counsel to troubled hearts.
    1. A troubled heart manifests itself in different ways.
        a. When our spirits are agitated and our world seems to be falling apart
        b. When life overwhelms us and our circumstances are out of control
    2. An untroubled heart remains possible in all of life's circumstances.
        a. It distinguishes us from non-Christians
        b. It involves a heavenly poise that marks us out as different
    3. A troubled heart reveals an underlying problem.
        a. Seeing difficulties as too great
        b. Seeing resources as too small
    4. A troubled heart can be avoided even if troubles cannot.
        a. We overcome them through the victory of Jesus (see John 16:33).
        b. We overcome them through our trust in Jesus (see Mark 4:40).
    5. We should not let our hearts be troubled.
        a. Looking to Christ as our refuge
        b. Looking to Christ as our Savior
        c. Remembering Christ as the way to heaven

B. Jesus makes a gospel-centered response to troubled Thomas.
    1. Thomas does not know where Jesus is going, so how can he know the way there?
    2. Thomas is a pessimist failing to see Jesus for who He is.
    3. Response: *I am the way to the Father* (John 14:6).
        a. Not found in the law but in Him to whom it points, for the former is the shadow and the latter the reality of grace (see John 1:14, 17; Heb. 10:1)
        b. Exclusively in Him, the way, the truth, and the life
    4. If there was another way to save us than for His Son to die, our Heavenly Father would have found it.

C. Jesus makes a gospel-centered response to troubled Philip.
    1. He wants to see the Father, which will be enough (John 14:8).
    2. He is a self-sufficient operator trying to work things out without reference to Jesus.
    3. Response: *Whoever has seen me has seen the Father* (John 14:9).
        a. Not One who is the Father
        b. But the One who reveals the Father
    4. Through Jesus, we are able to call God our "heavenly Father."

STUDY QUESTIONS

1. The use of "Do not let your hearts be troubled" (John 14:1) at funerals is usually done without a proper reference to the context before it.
    a. True
    b. False

2. A troubled heart indicates primarily a spirit of depression.
    a. True
    b. False

3. Which passage teaches that we overcome a troubled heart through the victory of Jesus?
    a. John 14:9
    b. Mark 4:40
    c. John 16:33
    d. John 14:6

4. Which passage teaches that we overcome a troubled heart through trust in Jesus?
    a. John 14:9
    b. Mark 4:40
    c. John 16:33
    d. John 14:6

5. Which passage teaches that Thomas needed to realize that Jesus alone is the way to God the Father?
    a. John 14:9
    b. Mark 4:40
    c. John 16:33
    d. John 14:6

6. Which passage teaches that Philip needed to realize that whoever has seen the Son has seen the Father?
    a. John 14:9
    b. Mark 4:40
    c. John 16:33
    d. John 14:6

7. The underlying problem for a troubled heart is:
    a. Seeing our trials as too large
    b. Seeing our resources as too small
    c. Seeing our resolve as too weak
    d. Both a and b
    e. Both b and c

BIBLE STUDY

1. Based on his call to have courage in the face of persecution in 1 Peter 3:14, it's clear that Peter understood the call not to be agitated. What does he see as the key to put off the spirit of fear in 1 Peter 3:15?

2. John 14:6 comes in answer to Thomas' question about the "way," so this verse has its primary focus on Jesus alone being the way to God. The terms *truth* and *life* come alongside to bolster this idea as if to communicate the following: "Jesus is the only way to Father, since He alone is the truth and the life." From all this and previous lessons and your knowledge of the gospel of John, discuss how Jesus, the "I Am," uses "truth" and "life" to support His role as the "way." Consider here just the testimony of John 1, 5, and 6 (John 1:4, 14, 17; 5:21, 24, 26; 6:40, 47–48, 63, 68).

3. From the lesson and reflection on John 1:14, 17 and Hebrews 10:1, how can the idea that the "law was given through Moses; grace and truth came through Jesus Christ," be easily misunderstood? Describe what this idea means as though you were explaining it to a child.

DISCUSSION QUESTIONS

1. When we say that Jesus was troubled that we may not be, why must we be careful not to identify our "troubled" hearts too closely with Jesus'?

2. Within our pluralistic society, believe it or not, many people who call themselves evangelicals would have no difficulty accepting the idea that Christians, Jews, Muslims, Hindus, and Buddhists all pray to the same God. Respond to this idea with Jesus' claim: "I am the way, and the truth, and the life. No one comes to the Father except through me." How does this statement disprove the idea that all people serve the same God?

3. In connection with the exclusive claim of Jesus above, Dr. Ferguson mentions that if our heavenly Father could have found another "way" to save us than to put His Son to death, He would found it. How then is a postmodern response such as "you have your way and I have mine" a slap in the face of God? How would you graciously answer such a response?

APPLICATION

1. How can focusing on the troubled heart Jesus endured help us with our own troubled hearts? In answering this, reflect upon Dr. Ferguson's observation that for troubled hearts, our trials are seen as too great and God's resources as too small.

2. Why must we continually remind ourselves of the truth of John 14:6? How would a regular reflection on each of the terms "way," "truth," and "life," help us?

3. In the spirit of 1 John 3:1, "See what kind of love the Father has given to us, that we should be called children of God," meditate on how amazing it is that through Jesus we have access to God as our heavenly Father. If we are in Christ, we belong to the Father and He loves us as His children. How should this affect the way we approach God in prayer as "Our Father in heaven" (Matt. 6:9–13)?

FOR FURTHER STUDY

R.C. Sproul, *The Prayer of the Lord*
R.C. Sproul, *Who Is Jesus?*
Sinclair B. Ferguson, *In Christ Alone*

6

It Is Better
That Another Comes

MESSAGE INTRODUCTION

Martin Luther's students often conversed over dinner with him and recorded many of his comments in what became known as *Table Talk*. In this lesson, Dr. Ferguson speaks of the "table talk" of Jesus that John recorded in the Upper Room Discourse. In this passage, the Savior discusses the advantage for the disciples when He leaves them and sends "another Helper" (14:16), the Holy Spirit. The disciples could not, however, agree that the promised Spirit would make up for the bodily absence of Christ. Only later would the disciples fully realize the vital role of the Spirit to take up the work of Christ as Teacher, Counselor, and Homemaker.

SCRIPTURE READINGS

John 14:16–31; 1 Corinthians 2:9–14

LEARNING OBJECTIVES

1. To recognize the role of the Holy Spirit to carry on the work of Christ in believers
2. To understand the function of the Holy Spirit as teacher, counselor, and homemaker
3. To realize the importance of the Holy Spirit's ministry in connection to the believer's fellowship with the Father and Son

QUOTATION

It is the Holy Spirit who supplies the bodily absence of Christ. Hence some of the ancients call him . . . the Vicar of Christ; he who represents his person, and discharges his promised work . . . He so represents the Person, and supplies the bodily absence of Christ, that on his presence the being of the Church, the success of the ministry, and the edification of the whole absolutely depend. Now who that has any affection for Christ, does not think that the bodily presence of Christ would be of unspeakable advantage to him? And so no doubt it would had any such thing been appointed in the wisdom and love of God. But so it is not; and we are taught to expect more advantage and benefit by his spiritual presence with us by the Holy Ghost; it is better and more expedient for us.

—John Owen

LECTURE OUTLINE

A. The Holy Spirit assumes the role of Teacher.
   1. Jesus taught the disciples (e.g. John 14:23–25).
   2. The coming Holy Spirit would do the same (John 14:26).
   3. The Holy Spirit makes known the deep things of God better than before (see 1 Cor. 2:10).
   4. The Holy Spirit allows disciples "in Christ" to know Christ "in them" even better (John 14:17; see also Rom. 8:8–10 and Col. 1:27).

B. The Holy Spirit assumes the role of Counselor.
   1. Jesus filled the role of Counselor for His disciples (e.g. Thomas, John 14:5; Philip, John 14:8; Judas [not Iscariot], John 14:22).
   2. The coming Holy Spirit would do the same (John 14:16).
   3. The term *counselor*, or paraclete, refers to the legal world.
      a. Prosecuting counsel bringing conviction (see John 16:8)
      b. Advocating counsel pleading the cause of Christ in our lives
   4. Such counsel from the Spirit comes in both a legal and a relational sense.
      a. One who knows Christ most intimately
      b. One who knows Christians most intimately

C. The Holy Spirit assumes the role of Homemaker.
   1. Jesus filled the role of Homemaker for His disciples (e.g. John 14:2, 3).
   2. The coming Holy Spirit would do the same (John 14:18, 23).
      a. Not leaving us as orphans
      b. Making a dwelling place for the Father and Son
   3. The wonder of the Spirit's ministry is to make the Father and Son feel at home in our hearts.

STUDY QUESTIONS

   1. The Holy Spirit would allow the disciples to know Jesus better than they did when He was bodily present with them.
      a. True
      b. False

2. The term *counselor,* or paraclete, should be understood in a strictly legal sense.
    a. True
    b. False

3. That the Holy Spirit is called "another Helper" does not mean He is different than Jesus so much as it refers to His making up for the bodily absence of Christ.
    a. True
    b. False

4. The Holy Spirit would assume the role of Teacher as mentioned in:
    a. John 14:16
    b. John 14:18, 23
    c. John 14:26
    d. 1 Cor. 2:10

5. The Holy Spirit would teach the disciples the deep things of God better than ever as mentioned in:
    a. John 14:16
    b. John 14:18, 23
    c. John 14:26
    d. 1 Cor. 2:10

6. The Holy Spirit would come as another Helper or Counselor as mentioned in:
    a. John 14:16
    b. John 14:18, 23
    c. John 14:26
    d. 1 Cor. 2:10

7. Jesus would come by way of the Holy Spirit to the disciples and not leave them as orphans as seen in:
    a. John 14:16
    b. John 14:18, 23
    c. John 14:26
    d. 1 Cor. 2:10

8. The Holy Spirit's role as Counselor refers to:
    a. A prosecutor bringing conviction
    b. An advocate pleading the cause of Christ
    c. A friend who knows Christ and us the best
    d. Both a and b
    e. All of the above

BIBLE STUDY

1. Examine 1 Corinthians 2:9–14. As it relates to the truth of God's Word, what does the Spirit do in the connection of God as the revealer of truth and believers as the recipients of truth? What about those who are not in Christ?

2. Reflect upon Romans 8:8–10 and Colossians 1:27 in light of John 14:17. What is the dynamic relationship between Christ, the Spirit, and believers set forth in these verses? How does it help to verify Christ's claim that His bodily absence is better for the disciples?

3. Examine John 14:18 and 23 in their context. In Dr. Ferguson's book *The Holy Spirit*, he says of John 14:18: "When Jesus announces his departure from the disciples but assures them that 'I will come [back] to you' (14:18), he is speaking neither about his resurrection reappearance (20:14, 19), nor about his anticipated final return, but about his 'coming' in the gift of the Spirit. So complete is the union between Jesus and the Paraclete that the coming of the latter is the coming of Jesus himself in the Spirit." Not all agree with this interpretation of the "coming." However, given the mysterious interaction between Christ and the Spirit in relation to the believer as seen in the previous question, can you see this as a legitimate approach to these verses? Consider it in light of 1 Corinthians 15:45 and 2 Corinthians 3:17 (see also the John Owen quote above).

DISCUSSION QUESTIONS

1. In light of the Spirit searching the deep things of God and then teaching them to us, how should this affect a Christian's approach to interpreting the Scriptures, from reading one's devotions, to listening to sermons, to teaching or preaching from God's Word?

2. The "orphans" mentioned in John 14:18 evoke the image of mourning or abandoned offspring without parents. Given that Christ comes by way of the Spirit to prevent abandonment after His bodily absence, how can we use this passage to bring the balm of the gospel to a world full of wrecked relationships?

APPLICATION

1. Give consideration to your own understanding of the Scriptures as you read the Bible and hear it read and preached. Recognizing that the truth of God is spiritually discerned, do you enter into these activities with a conscious dependence on the Holy Spirit as your teacher? Why is it so easy to barge into such things in the flesh? Ask the Spirit Himself to turn you away from such a tendency.

2. Reflect upon the Spirit's role to plead the cause of Christ as both an Advocate (knowing Christ and us so well) and a Prosecutor (convicting us of sin, righteousness, and judgment). Think of one way concretely that these roles provide both a comfort and a warning in your life personally or in someone else's life to whom you are ministering.

3. Reflect upon the Spirit's role as a Homemaker in your life. Are you focusing on living the Christian life in a way that seeks to make the Father and Son feel welcome in your heart?

FOR FURTHER STUDY

Sinclair B. Ferguson, *The Holy Spirit*
John Owen, *A Discourse Concerning the Holy Spirit*

7

Abiding in the Vine

MESSAGE INTRODUCTION

Did you know that the most common description in the New Testament for believers is not "Christian" but simply "in Christ"? Through the power of the Holy Spirit, believers experience the indwelling of Christ. The disciples struggled to grasp the advantage of this special and mysterious union and how powerfully present a bodily absent Christ was in it. To help His disciples lay hold of this concept, Jesus uses the picture of a vine and its branches. In this lesson, Dr. Ferguson opens up this image from John 15 emphasizing the significance of our union with Christ as we abide in Him, the True Vine.

SCRIPTURE READINGS

John 15:1–17; Galatians 2:20

LEARNING OBJECTIVES

1. To understand what it means to abide in Christ, the True Vine
2. To identify the connection between the Son as the Vine, the Father as the Gardener, and believers as the branches
3. To recognize that the believer's source of nourishment and fruitfulness is in Christ and His Spirit-empowered Word

QUOTATION

For the relation of the branches to the vine is such that they contribute nothing to the vine, but from it derive their own means of life; while that of the vine to the branches is such that it supplies their vital nourishment, and receives nothing from them. And so their having Christ abiding in them, and abiding themselves in Christ, are in both respects advantageous, not to Christ, but to the disciples. For when the branch is cut off, another may spring up from the living root; but that which is cut off cannot live apart from the root.

—Augustine

LECTURE OUTLINE

A. The source of fruitfulness is found in union with the Vine (John 15:1, 4, 5).

   1. Jesus as the Vine cleansed believers as the branches that they may bear fruit (John 15:3).

   2. The branches bear fruit because they are in union with the Vine, the source of life.

   3. Apart from the Vine, the branches can bear nothing (John 15:5).

   4. The branches must "abide" in the Vine to bear fruit.

      a. Referring to our union with Christ as the source of all life

      b. Referring to life by faith in Christ who gave Himself for us (Gal. 2:20)

B. The branches will be pruned by the Father (John 15:1, 2, 6).

   1. The idea of pruning or "cutting back" branches of a vine to make them more fruitful seems strange to many people.

   2. Using this image for disciples as branches is even more difficult to grasp.

      a. Branches pruned by the Father Himself as the Vinedresser

      b. Branches either cultivated for fruitfulness or cut off to die (see also Luke 13:6–9)

      c. Branches that are living and responding

      d. Branches that feel pain and wonder, "Why are you doing that?"

   3. The pruning of disciples will be mysterious and make them sore.

      a. Without the Father making a mistake

      b. Without the Father wasting anything He cuts away

      c. With the Father always concerned for our fruitfulness

C. The branches will be nourished by the Word (John 15:7, 10).

   1. Jesus abides in the branches by way of His Word dwelling in them richly (see Col. 3:16).

      a. Soaking in the Word of God

      b. Leaving no room locked to the Word

      c. Flowing "bibline" when pricked as Spurgeon said of Bunyan

   2. The Word nourishes us not by us making it work but through its work in us (1 Thess. 2:13).

   3. The church today has little room for the Word and suffers from malnourishment.

      a. Fostering spiritual anemia

      b. Lacking in "vitamin W," the Word

D. The most important fruit of the branches is love (John 15:8–13, 16–17).

   1. Abiding in Christ involves abiding in His love and expressing it toward God and others.

   2. We do not have such love in us, for it comes from abiding in Christ.

STUDY QUESTIONS

1. The most common description for believers in the New Testament is "Christian."
    a. True
    b. False

2. Jesus used the image of a vine to teach His disciples that without Him they can do nothing.
    a. True
    b. False

3. The idea that something not bearing fruit is cut off and thrown in the fire is seen in:
    a. Galatians 2:20
    b. Luke 13:6–9
    c. Colossians 3:16
    d. 1 Thessalonians 2:13

4. The idea that the Word of God is at work in us is seen in:
    a. Galatians 2:20
    b. Luke 13:6–9
    c. Colossians 3:16
    d. 1 Thessalonians 2:13

5. The idea that the life we live, we do so by our faith in Christ is seen in:
    a. Galatians 2:20
    b. Luke 13:6–9
    c. Colossians 3:16
    d. 1 Thessalonians 2:13

6. The idea that the Word of Christ abides or dwells in us richly is seen in:
    a. Galatians 2:20
    b. Luke 13:6–9
    c. Colossians 3:16
    d. 1 Thessalonians 2:13

7. Believers' abiding in the vine refers to their:
    a. Sharing humanity with Christ
    b. Union with Christ
    c. Faith in Christ
    d. Both a and b
    e. Both b and c

8. Jesus used the image of a vine to teach His disciples something of:
   a. The mysterious union they would experience with Him
   b. The advantage of His bodily absence
   c. The powerful indwelling of Christ through the Holy Spirit
   d. Both a and b
   e. All of the above

BIBLE STUDY

1. Examine Galatians 2:20. What two implications (present in the verse) should we draw from Paul's admission, "It is no longer I who live"? What does this mean for the Christian life and the idea of being in union with Christ?

2. Study the parable of the barren fig tree in Luke 13:6–9, which sets forth the warning of impending judgment upon unrepentant and unfruitful Israel. Yet, what is it that you observe with the plea to wait before cutting it down? What hope does that give you regarding the lack of fruit often observed in the church? (see 2 Peter 3:9).

3. When we consider the working or effectual Word in believers as mentioned in 1 Thessalonians 2:13, what is the connection of this idea to the Thessalonians receiving this as the Word of God in the first place? What encouragement does this give in the ministry of preaching and evangelizing?

DISCUSSION QUESTIONS

1. Regarding the suffering of Amy Carmichael in her ministry in India, Dr. Ferguson quotes her as saying, "What a prodigal waste it appears to see scattered on the floor the bright green leaves and the bare stem bleeding in a hundred places from the sharp knife. But with a tried and trusted husbandman, there is not a random stroke in it all, nothing cut away which it would not have been a loss to keep and gain to lose." Read through this statement carefully. What does it say about the Father's pruning activity from the perspective of the world and the church?

2. Dr. Ferguson attests that modern Christians think that the Christian life is largely of our own doing (for example, looking for counsel and advice to enable us to do the Christian life better). "But the biblical perspective is somewhat different from that," he argues. "The biblical perspective is that first and foremost, we need to let the Word of God do its own work in us." How should this prompt anyone sitting under the ministry of the Word to respond?

3. Dr. Ferguson mentions Spurgeon's testimony of the Bible-saturated life and ministry of John Bunyan. Here is a fuller quote: "Read anything of his, and you will see that it is almost like reading the Bible itself. . . . Why, this man is a living

Bible! Prick him anywhere—his blood is Bibline, the very essence of the Bible flows from him. He cannot speak without quoting a text, for his very soul is full of the Word of God." While we cannot make the Word of God work in us, what does this quote tell us that Christians can do?

APPLICATION

1. Reflect on the idea that the New Testament much more frequently describes believers as "in Christ" rather than as "Christians." If you were able to keep this concept "in Christ" with you all the time, what kind of impact do you think it would have on how you view yourself and others?

2. Dr. Ferguson mentions the fact that the church has little patience for longer and more frequent sermons, as we suffer from spiritual anemia and a lack of "vitamin W" (the Word). Why do you think this is the case? Is this the case for you?

3. The idea of abiding in Christ by letting His word abide or dwell in us richly implies the necessity of soaking in that Word on a regular basis. How can you foster such a "soaking"?

FOR FURTHER STUDY

John Bunyan, *The Barren Fig Tree*
Matthew Henry, *Directions for Daily Communion with God*
John Owen, *Of Communion with God the Father, Son and Holy Spirit*
David Murray, *How Sermons Work*
Steven J. Lawson, *Feed My Sheep*

8

Hated but Helped

MESSAGE INTRODUCTION

Some argue that the history of Western philosophy can primarily be summed up as a footnote to the thought of Plato. We can say that the entire Bible shows a similar connection to Genesis 3:15, which announces the enmity between the seed of the woman and the seed of the serpent. In John 15:18–27, and in connection to this ongoing conflict, Jesus recognizes that the time has come for the climactic battle between the two seeds or kingdoms, one that would take Him to the cross. However, His very death would crush the one who has the power of death, the devil. In this lesson, Dr. Ferguson shows us from this passage how the disciples are caught up in the war. They too will be hated by the world, yet also helped by the One who overcomes the world.

SCRIPTURE READINGS

John 15:18–27

LEARNING OBJECTIVES

1. To realize that the followers of Christ will experience opposition just as He has
2. To recognize the opposition for what it is as Jesus exposes it
3. To respond properly to the opposition in light of the truth about it and our resources against it

QUOTATION

From the beginning (Gen. 3:15), the Lord Himself placed an inveterate enmity between the serpent and the Savior and those belonging to the one or the other, and in proportion as the disciples of Christ follow His example, walk as He walked, reflect His image, will they be opposed by Satan and his seed. "If the world hate you, ye know that it hated Me before it hated you. . . . The servant is not greater than his lord. If they have persecuted Me, they will also persecute you" (John 15:18, 20). God has predestinated His children "to be conformed to the image of His Son" (Romans 8:29): first in holiness, then in suffering, afterward in glory. Scripture reveals the solemn fact that the Christian is menaced by deadly foes, who will show him no quarter nor relax in their efforts to destroy him.

—A.W. Pink

LECTURE OUTLINE

A. Jesus gives reasons for the opposition that His followers face.
  1. We sometimes respond wrongly and stir up antagonism unnecessarily.
     a. For acting foolishly
     b. For speaking rashly
  2. There exists an ongoing opposition to those who belong to Christ (see Gen. 3:15).
  3. When we are united to Christ, we will be hated as He was (John 15:18–20).
     a. Anticipating this as followers of Christ
     b. Possessing a proper understanding of what it means to follow Christ
     c. Not being surprised as though something was going wrong
     d. Recognizing that something may be going very right
  4. The book of Acts makes it clear that we will face it.
     a. Showing us not only the glorious fruitfulness but also the shameful antagonism
     b. Granting us the principle "Forewarned is forearmed"
     c. Leaving us with examples of joyful fellowship in the sufferings of Christ
  5. We do not belong to the world (John 15:18, 19).
  6. The servant is not greater than the master (John 15:20; see also John 13:16).

B. Jesus unmasks the opposition that His followers face.
  1. The opposition does not know the Father, but we do (John 15:21).
     a. Seeming so big but not really
     b. Prompting our pity in the end
  2. The opposition will face judgment, but we will not (John 15:22, 24).
     a. Impending doom awaiting them
     b. Prompting our courage in the end
  3. The opposition does not catch us by surprise.
     a. Understanding that they come necessarily
     b. Prompting us to await them while standing tall

C. Jesus and His disciples must respond to the opposition they face (John 15:26–27).
  1. We recognize that the Spirit in His coming bears witness to Christ.
  2. His disciples will also bear witness of Him as they are united to Him.
     a. Emboldening our witness
     b. Drawing opponents to become friends (e.g. Stephen before Saul, Acts 7)

STUDY QUESTIONS

1. In some sense, the entire Bible is a footnote to Genesis 3:15.
    a. True
    b. False

2. Sometimes Christians bring on opposition for the wrong reasons.
    a. True
    b. False

3. It is more proper to say that the disciples in Acts rejoiced in suffering rather than the fellowship they had with Christ in the midst of it.
    a. True
    b. False

4. Regarding the persecution promised by Jesus, "Forewarned is _____."
    a. Forecasted
    b. Foreknown
    c. Forearmed
    d. Foretold

5. That Jesus _____ the opposition we face prompts courage to face it.
    a. Conquers
    b. Rebukes
    c. Loves
    d. Unmasks

6. We are prompted to _____, because the opposition does not know the Father.
    a. Pity
    b. Courage
    c. Understanding
    d. Rejoice

7. The Book of Acts makes it clear that we will face persecution as Jesus promised, _____.
    a. Showing us that we should eagerly seek persecution
    b. Leaving us with examples of fellowship in the sufferings of Christ
    c. Granting us the principle "Forebearing is forewarning"
    d. Both a and b
    e. Both b and c

8. When we are united to Christ, we will be hated as He was and should _____.
   a. Anticipate such treatment
   b. Recognize that it may come because something is going very right
   c. Not be surprised though things are going very wrong
   d. Both a and b
   e. Both b and c

BIBLE STUDY

1. In John 14:12, Jesus promised that His disciples would do greater things than He, referring to the preaching of the gospel in the power of the Spirit. We see this fulfilled in Acts 2 when Peter preaches at Pentecost and thousands are converted. How do we reconcile this success with the persecution faced later on in Acts?

2. In Acts 5:41, we read that the apostles left the Sanhedrin "rejoicing that they were counted worthy to suffer dishonor for the name." How do we rescue the Apostles from the charge that such an attitude is masochistic?

3. In relation to persecution that comes to the followers of Christ, Jesus asserts, "Remember the word that I said to you: A servant is not greater than his master. If they persecuted me, they will also persecute you" (John 15:20). Obviously, the context is different than his prior use of this statement in John 13:16. However, given that we read, "Remember the word I said to you," it seems that Jesus links the two uses to some degree. How are the two uses alike and how are they different?

DISCUSSION QUESTIONS

1. What does "Forewarned is forearmed" mean? Dr. Ferguson then uses this statement in connection with the assertion that we should not "expect a Christian life or the community life of the church ever to be without opposition and antagonism," because we do not belong to the world. What does this mean and what does it say to our constant striving for the world's acceptance?

2. "Intimidation is one of the key instruments that Satan uses," Dr. Ferguson says, "in order to close our mouths and to shut down our Christian witness because we see the opposition as large and we become like little church mice." How should the church respond to such a tendency?

3. While we know that the followers of Jesus will experience persecution as He did, why is the church continually caught by surprise?

APPLICATION

1. Christians have a tendency to wag their heads at people in the world who want nothing to do with Christ, especially those who mock and despise our Christian faith. Ask your heavenly Father to grant you the ability to pity these people instead as you consider the judgment that awaits them.

2. Jesus says that you are not of this world and so the world will persecute you. Take stock of your life. Do you find the tendency to be as much like the world as possible so that you do not stand out like a sore thumb? While Jesus does not expect you to unnecessarily alienate people, what can you do to counter the tendency to be conformed to the world?

3. Reflect on the privilege that it is to bear witness for Christ as His representative. Pray that He would embolden you to witness for Him and even use the very opposition you endure to draw someone to Himself.

FOR FURTHER STUDY

Thomas Boston, *The Art of Man-Fishing*
William Gurnall, *The Christian in Complete Armor*

9

Getting inside Their Heads

MESSAGE INTRODUCTION

So far in this series, the Upper Room Discourse has taken the disciples on a roller coaster of emotions, especially with the pronouncement of betrayal and denial within the inner circle of disciples. If that was not enough, Jesus would depart from them and leave behind terrible opposition that was supposed to be of no surprise. Now, He says that He has many more things to tell them, but they "cannot bear them now" (John 16:12). Jesus does not overwhelm them with more, but does remind them that the Holy Spirit as Counselor will guide them in all the truths that will be revealed later. Jesus now addresses them as though He were answering their unspoken questions. In this lesson, Dr. Ferguson deals with important questions and the answers Christ lovingly and sensitively gives.

SCRIPTURE READINGS

John 16:1–15

LEARNING OBJECTIVES

1. To recognize that the teaching of Christ is a preservative against falling away
2. To realize that, as the Spirit helps us through the Word of Christ, we bear witness to Christ Himself
3. To appreciate the fact that Christ in His wisdom withholds the details of the future from us for the good of His disciples

QUOTATION

No man can know Jesus Christ unless he is taught of God. There is no doctrine of the Bible which can be safely, thoroughly, and truly learned, except by the agency of the one authoritative teacher. Ah! tell me not of systems of divinity; tell me not of schemes of theology; tell me not of infallible commentators, or most learned and most arrogant doctors; but tell me of the Great Teacher, who shall instruct us, the sons of God, and shall make us wise to understand all things. He is the Teacher; it matters not what this or that man says; I rest on no man's boasting authority, nor will you. Ye are not to be carried away with the craftiness of men, nor sleight of words; this is the authoritative oracle, the Holy Ghost resting in the hearts of his children.

—C.H. Spurgeon

LECTURE OUTLINE

A. Why are you telling us these things now?
   1. So His joy would be in them and their joy would be full (John 15:11).
   2. He also told these things now to keep them from falling away (John 16:1).
      a. "Do not let your hearts be troubled"
      b. "The Holy Spirit will come to be your Helper"
   3. The hour of darkness was coming and they needed to hear these things (John 16:4).

B. Why did you not tell us these things before?
   1. He did not tell them because He was with them.
   2. He did not tell them because each day has enough of its own trouble (Matt. 6:34).
   3. He was safeguarding them from a burden they were not yet able to bear.
      a. Protecting them from the future (see Matt. 6:34)
      b. Protecting them from being distracted (see Isa. 40:11)

C. Why are you going away?
   1. He was going away for the advantage of the world through the coming Holy Spirit.
      a. Convicting the world (John 16:8–11)
      b. Causing greater results than when Jesus was bodily present (John 14:12)
      c. Bringing glory to the Savior in the conversion of sinners (Acts 2:41)
   2. He was going away for the advantage of the disciples through the coming Holy Spirit (John 16:12–15).
      a. Getting inside their minds to guide them away from the confusion
      b. Opening their eyes to the truth of His glory
      c. Leading them into a greater knowledge of Jesus
      d. Leading them into greater fellowship with all three persons of the Trinity

STUDY QUESTIONS

1. Jesus rebukes the disciples for the fact that they cannot bear all that He has to tell them.
   a. True
   b. False

2. Jesus at times anticipated the questions of His disciples, then answered them.
    a. True
    b. False

3. To the question, "Why are you telling us these things now?" Jesus answered:
    a. Because I was with you
    b. To keep you from falling away
    c. For the advantage of the world
    d. Each day has its own trouble

4. To the question, "Why did you not tell us these things before?" Jesus answered:
    a. Because I was with you
    b. To keep you from falling away
    c. For the advantage of the world
    d. So My joy would be in you

5. To the question, "Why are you leaving us?" Jesus answered:
    a. Because I was with you
    b. To keep you from falling away
    c. For the advantage of the world
    d. Each day has its own trouble

6. The Holy Spirit was coming to convict the _____ of sin, righteousness, and judgment.
    a. Church
    b. Disciples
    c. World
    d. Jews

7. The coming Holy Spirit would be of advantage to the world for the following reasons:
    a. Convicting of sin, righteousness, and judgment
    b. Causing greater results than when Jesus was bodily present
    c. Bringing glory to the Savior in the conversion of sinners
    d. Both a and b
    e. All of the above

8. The coming Holy Spirit would be of advantage to the disciples for the following reasons:
    a. Leading them into a greater knowledge of Jesus
    b. Leading them into greater fellowship with the Godhead
    c. Allowing them to perform greater miracles of healing
    d. Both a and b
    e. All of the above

BIBLE STUDY

1. Examine Matthew 6:34 in light of Jesus' mentioning troubles in John 16:1 ("these things") that certainly extend beyond that day. How do we reconcile these two verses, since the former seems to say, "Just focus on the day at hand"?

2. Regarding the advantage of the Holy Spirit to the world, what is the connection between the mass conversion in Acts 2 and the greater things promised in John 14:12? What is the key phrase in this verse for a right understanding of it? How do these verses relate to the victorious promise mentioned in Matthew 16:18? In answering this, it is vital to reflect upon Matthew 16:21.

3. In Dr. Ferguson's book *The Holy Spirit,* he observes the connection between the promise in John 16:8–11 and fulfillment in Acts 2:22–24. Thus, the truth of Christ's exaltation (in fulfillment of Joel 2:28; Ps. 16:8–11; 110:1) is manifested by the Spirit's convicting Peter's hearers of sin, righteousness, and judgment. Note how Peter's sermon focuses on this threefold conviction in Acts 2:22–24.

DISCUSSION QUESTIONS

1. Think of a situation in which you had sad news and chose to limit it or not to share it at all with a young child. Why did you withhold such information? How does this help you understand the approach of Jesus to His disciples? How does He continue to approach us in this way today?

2. Dr. Ferguson relates the principle "We cannot have tomorrow's grace before the day dawns." In light of Jesus' withholding things from His disciples for their protection, how should this principle instruct Christians individually and the church corporately?

3. Dr. Ferguson calls attention the Irish monk Brendan of Birr of the sixth century, who was asked by the pagan King Brude, "If I believe your message, and become Christ's man, what shall I find?" Brendan replied, "You shall stumble upon wonder upon wonder—and every wonder true!" In light of this lesson and the ministry of the Holy Spirit, explain what this response means.

APPLICATION

1. Why is it that we struggle so much to make sense of every trial that comes into our lives? It seems, as well, when we do not have all of our questions answered by God, that we can so easily question Him and the justice of what is going on. How can this lesson and the truths of the passage at hand be used as a safeguard against that?

2. We may never preach a Pentecost sermon, but we have the Holy Spirit to guide us into the truth, which in turn is used to convict others. With the powerful working of the Spirit pleading the cause of Christ, we can take heart when witnessing to others. We can lay aside the mentality that says, "It is of no use to share the gospel with such a person; he will never come to Christ." Would we not have said the same thing of the Apostle Paul?

3. How did the Brendan quote affect you? Have you experienced this truth in the Christian life as you, perhaps for years and years, keep stumbling upon wonder after wonder? This ought to be the case for every child of God guided in the way of truth by the Holy Spirit. Let us lay hold of the psalmist's burden to cry out for such wonders, "Open my eyes, that I may behold wondrous things out of your law" (Ps. 119:18).

FOR FURTHER STUDY

Sinclair B. Ferguson, *The Holy Spirit*
R.C. Sproul, *The Mystery of the Holy Spirit*
C.H. Spurgeon, "The Comforter," a sermon delivered on January 23, 1855

10

The Meaning
of Christmas at Easter

MESSAGE INTRODUCTION

Preachers sometimes speak over the heads of people and so fail to connect with them. As Charles Spurgeon once observed, "Jesus said, 'Feed my sheep,' not my giraffes." Yet, our Savior at times delivered teachings that puzzled His disciples, and He even withheld things they could not yet bear. This does not mean that Christ lacked clarity but that the disciples lacked spiritual discernment. As Dr. Ferguson argues, they needed "Velcro strips" in their thinking so that the truth would stick. In this lesson, we find Jesus patiently leading them into deeper truth as He responds to key questions Yet, it would take time for everything to make sense to them. Like the economic forecaster who said of holiday profits, "The meaning of Christmas will not become clear until Easter," Jesus' teaching concerning Himself would not be totally clear until the resurrection.

SCRIPTURE READINGS

John 16:16–33; Luke 24:24, 25

LEARNING OBJECTIVES

1. To see Jesus as a patient and sensitive teacher who leads His followers into the truth
2. To recognize that suffering for Christ and His followers is productive of joy
3. To realize that tribulation cannot be avoided for Christians, but defeat can

QUOTATION

He overcame the world in his personal conflict, and by his death. Now the victory of Christ our head concerns his members; for he did not overcome the world for himself, but for us: (1 Cor. 15:57), "But thanks be to God, who gives us the victory through our

Lord Jesus Christ." He overcame the world in our name, and when we are interested in him, he makes us conquerors together with himself, and in all our conflicts and sufferings assures us of a certain victory. So that his suffering people need not be dismayed with the power and policy, the threats and terrors of the world, for though Christ will not exempt them from a battle and exercise, yet they are partakers of his victory by faith, and, abiding in him, find they have to do with enemies already vanquished.

—Thomas Manton

LECTURE OUTLINE

A. What is all this talk about a little while? (John 16:16)
   1. In a little while, He will be taken from them for His crucifixion.
   2. A little while later, He will reappear to them in the resurrection.
   3. "The meaning of Christmas will not become clear until Easter."
      a. An economic forecast of the real success of Christmas sales seen at Easter
      b. Related to the meaning of Jesus' life made clear at His resurrection
   4. The disciples were working with a resurrection-less gospel.
      a. Seeing only opposition and difficulty
      b. Being filled with fear
   5. Joy will follow the sorrow as with a woman in labor.
      a. Not just joy following the pain
      b. But also pain being essential to the joy
   6. For the Christ and those who follow Him, pain is productive of glory and the joy that attends it (see Luke 24:24, 25; 2 Cor. 4:17).

B. Why is it that Jesus seems to be speaking to us in riddles? (John 16:25)
   1. He had just used an illustration of a woman in labor.
   2. The figure of speech was used to help them understand what they were not grasping.
   3. The day is coming that He will speak plainly to them about the Father.
   4. This plain speech occurred at His resurrection (John 20:17).
   5. Upon His resurrection, understanding of the new relationship with the Father would become clearer.
      a. As they learn to go to Him directly (John 16:26)
      b. As they recognize His love for them (John 16:27)

C. How are you going to help us when you are distant from us? (John 16:29–33).
   1. He would be leaving them for this season.
   2. They would not see Him again in the season to come until they would be in glory.
   3. They say they understand now as He speaks plainly.
   4. The hour was coming when they would scatter from Him and leave Him.
   5. He was not alone, since the Father is with Him.
   6. He speaks to them to give them peace (16:33).

    a. In spite of the trouble they would face in this world
    b. In view of the fact that He has overcome the world

STUDY QUESTIONS

1. Jesus always spoke plainly to His disciples.
   a. True
   b. False

2. Jesus did not lack clarity when He taught, but His disciples did lack spiritual discernment.
   a. True
   b. False

3. Jesus' teaching concerning God would not become fully clear to the disciples until the resurrection.
   a. True
   b. False

4. Which passage says it was necessary for Christ to suffer before entering glory?
   a. Luke 24:26
   b. John 20:17
   c. 1 Corinthians 15:57
   d. 2 Corinthians 4:17

5. Which passage says the affliction is light and momentary compared to the eternal glory to come?
   a. Luke 24:26
   b. John 20:17
   c. 1 Corinthians 15:57
   d. 2 Corinthians 4:17

6. Which passage says go tell my brothers that I go to My Father and their Father?
   a. Luke 24:26
   b. John 20:17
   c. 1 Corinthians 15:57
   d. 2 Corinthians 4:17

7. Part of the struggle for the disciples was that they were working with a
   _____ gospel.
   a. Puzzling
   b. Piecemeal
   c. Resurrection-less
   d. Vague

8. Jesus was able to promise peace to His disciples:
   a. In spite of the trouble they would face in this world
   b. In view of the fact that He has overcome the world
   c. In light of the fact that the Father was with Him
   d. Both a and b
   e. All of the above

BIBLE STUDY

1. Jesus spoke to His disciples in riddles, but He said in John 16:25 that the day was coming that He would speak plainly to them. Given that we live after the resurrection, does the use of figures of speech or parables have a function for either those inside or outside the kingdom? Must preachers today simply speak plainly without the use of such things as images, metaphors, or illustrations? Study Mark 4:11–13 and consider the book of Revelation as you answer this question.

2. Examine 2 Corinthians 4:17 and the affliction and glory mentioned by Paul. What two terms does he use for each? What should be the result of the truth communicated in this verse (see 2 Cor. 4:16)?

3. Study John 3:16 as you reflect upon Dr. Ferguson's reference to the mistaken idea that the Father loves His children because Jesus died on the cross for them. What does he mean by this and how does John 3:16 refute it?

DISCUSSION QUESTIONS

1. In light of this lesson and the Spurgeon quote in the introduction, what should preachers learn from the teaching approach of Jesus Christ?

2. Given the idea that suffering is productive of glory and joy in the Christian life, do you think that Ignatius got it right when he said, "I am the wheat of God . . . let me be ground by the teeth of the wild beasts," that he may then "truly" be called a Christian? Or, did he have too much of a fascination with martyrdom?

3. Dr. Ferguson calls attention to the hymn, "Crown Him with Many Crowns," and the phrase, "Those wounds, yet visible above, in beauty glorified." In speaking of the ascended and glorified Christ, what does this statement mean and how does it bolster the thrust of this lesson?

APPLICATION

1. Reflect upon the idea that suffering is productive of glory as it relates to your own life. How is this different from the idea that that glory simply follows suffering for you? How should this affect your attitude toward suffering?

2. Dr. Ferguson exhorts us to focus on the fact that the love of the Father stands behind the death of Christ for us rather than coming as a result of it. How should this inform how you look at your heavenly Father and how readily you bask in His love?

3. What two reminders do we need to hear over and over again from John 16:33 and what should the result be for us?

FOR FURTHER STUDY

Thomas Boston, *The Crook in the Lot: The Sovereignty of God in the Trials, Tribulations & Troubles of this Life*

John Piper and Justin Taylor, *Suffering and the Sovereignty of God*

R.C. Sproul, *Surprised by Suffering*

11

Father, Glorify Your Son

MESSAGE INTRODUCTION

In churches, we often hold social gatherings in order to grow in our knowledge of one another. There is perhaps no other gathering where we get to know people better than the prayer meeting. There, we have the privilege, as we listen to others pray out loud, of having them reveal some of the deepest desires of their hearts. If we share such a privilege within the context of the church, then there could be no greater privilege for the disciples of Jesus than to listen to Him pray. In this lesson, as we come to the end of the Upper Room Discourse, Dr. Ferguson begins to open up the High Priestly Prayer of Jesus Christ, focusing first on the prayer of Jesus concerning Himself.

SCRIPTURE READINGS

John 17:1–5; Psalm 29

LEARNING OBJECTIVES

1. To see the heart of Jesus in His High Priestly Prayer to the Father
2. To recognize Jesus' self-proclamation of deity
3. To understand Jesus' claim to and petition for a return to the former glory hidden in His incarnation

QUOTATION

His first words are, "Father, the hour is come, glorify thy Son, that thy Son also may glorify thee." As this is his first request, we may suppose it to be his supreme request and desire, and what lie ultimately aimed at in all. We consider what follows to the end, all the rest that is said in the prayer, seems to be but an amplification of this great request.—On the whole, I think it is pretty manifest, that Jesus Christ sought the glory of God as his highest and last end.

—Jonathan Edwards

LECTURE OUTLINE

A. The hour has come for Jesus to be glorified (John 17:1).

  1. For Israel on the Day of Atonement, the high priest went through a ritual of prayer offering up petitions for himself, his family, and the nation—in that order.

  2. This high priestly prayer anticipates Jesus' making petitions for Himself (verses 1–5), His immediate circle of disciples (verses 6–19), and the entire church (verses 20–26).

  3. The context of the prayer for the arrived-at hour is a meal, like previous glimpses of glory when His time had not yet come.

    a. At the feast at Cana (John 2:4, 11)

    b. At the Feast of Booths (John 7:6, 18)

  4. Now, at this meal, the hour had come.

    a. In obedience to His death on the cross (Phil. 2:8)

    b. In fulfillment of all Old Testament promises (e.g. Is. 53; Ps. 16, 22)

    c. In ultimate realization of the promise of crushing victory in Genesis 3:15

B. Jesus offers up the request that He be glorified (John 17:1).

  1. For what is Jesus asking?

    a. That the glory of God would not be given to another (Isa. 42:8; 48:11)

    b. That the Father would glorify His Son

    c. That the Son would in turn glorify the Father

  2. What is this glory?

    a. The external expression of God's attributes and perfections

    b. The kaleidoscopic colorful burst of the magnificence of God's character

    c. Captured in Psalm 29 with the majestic and powerful thunder and lightning of the voice of God, prompting the people to cry, "Glory!"

    d. To be manifested in Jesus, revealed in previous glimpses (for example, Mark 4:41; 9:2–3)

    e. That owed to Jesus as His self-proclaimed deity manifests (John 17:2)

  3. Why did He pray this way?

    a. Because His glory had been hidden

    b. Because He had been living as an alien resident in the polluted atmosphere of the earth, a place where He has been demeaned (see Isa. 48:11)

    c. Because He was homesick for the glory He once possessed in the presence of the Father

STUDY QUESTIONS

  1. Listening to someone pray gives us a glimpse into some of the deepest desires of his or her heart.

    a. True

    b. False

2. The title High Priestly Prayer is not very fitting for Jesus' prayer.
    a. True
    b. False

3. Which passage says Jesus humbled Himself in obedience to death on a cross?
    a. Genesis 3:15
    b. Ezekiel 37
    c. Psalm 22
    d. Philippians 2:8

4. Which passage says the hour of suffering had come in fulfillment of Old Testament promises?
    a. Isaiah 48:11
    b. Isaiah 53:5
    c. John 2:4, 11
    d. Philippians 2:8

5. Which passage says God will not give His glory to another?
    a. Isaiah 48:11
    b. Isaiah 53:5
    c. John 2:4, 11
    d. Philippians 2:8

6. God's glory refers to the external expression of His _____ and perfections.
    a. Theophanies
    b. Attributes
    c. Works
    d. Wonders

7. Jesus prayed to be glorified because:
    a. His glory had been hidden.
    b. He had been living as an alien resident in a polluted atmosphere.
    c. He was homesick for the glory He once possessed.
    d. Both a and b
    e. All of the above

BIBLE STUDY

1. Dr. Ferguson mentions the glimpses of Christ's glory in John 2:4,11; John 7:6,18; the calming of the Sea of Galilee (Mark 4:41); and the transfiguration (Mark 9:2–3). We have already considered that such glimpses, in connection with John 1:14, anticipated this time in the final days of Jesus' life. Even in the midst of what we know as the humiliation of Christ (i.e. that he was born as a man under the law, underwent the miseries of life to the point of death and burial, endured the wrath of God), what do these glimpses tell us about the certainty of His glorification? How does this affect our reading of the Gospels and especially how we look at the suffering of Christ, who subjected Himself to the "polluted atmosphere" of this earth?

2. Dr. Ferguson mentions that "the hour" had come for Jesus to suffer in fulfillment (in part) of Isaiah 53:5 and ultimately of Genesis 3:15. What is the link between these two verses and how would such a connection contribute to Christ's rebuke of the disciples in Luke 24:25–27?

3. Read Psalm 29, which gives us a majestic expression of the glory of God, to which the people respond with exuberance. How does such an expression help you to understand the longing of Christ for a complete restoration of His former glory?

DISCUSSION QUESTIONS

1. Dr. Ferguson gives a sense of the petition of Jesus for the Father to glorify Him: "Father, I not only emptied myself into the incarnation but there is a sense in which I have hidden my majesty in the incarnation. Will you not now, by your power, unveil that majesty so men and women will see who I really am?" Put this idea in simple words as though you were explaining this to an eight year-old child.

2. As Dr. Ferguson notes, even many Christians tend to see pursuit of the glory of God as antithetical to our own good. Why is that? How is this idea seen as faulty from just this lesson?

3. Dr. Ferguson discusses an allegory of the incarnation that he started to write titled, "The Stranger and the Smokers." He summarizes it this way: "And the allegory was about someone who has lived in the penthouse suite who has been, as it were, served night and day in the purified and rarified atmosphere of the penthouse suite. And he comes down from the penthouse suite on the elevator, and the elevator doors opened, and there's a crowd of smokers there. And he has never breathed in smoke and they take him—they drag him from the elevator and they breathe on him and they smoke more and more. And they seek to stick their

cigarettes into his mouth, and they breathe into his eyes, and they seek to destroy him because he is not one of them—he is not like them. And here is this one who has never breathed polluted air." Open up the significance of each of the elements of this allegory as it relates to Christ, His incarnation, and His glory.

APPLICATION

1.   Given what Dr. Ferguson said about our hearts being revealed in prayer, what does your church hear from your heart?

2.   Dr. Ferguson refers to the homesickness of Jesus as He prays for a restoration of His former glory. How does this relate to the homesickness (or lack thereof) that Christians experience in light of Paul's longing to "be with Christ, for that is far better"? How can we cultivate such a longing?

3.   Go back to the allegory of the Stranger and Smokers for a minute. How much do you feel at home among the polluted atmosphere of the "smoking" world? Do you try to fit in? Is there a sense in which they recognize that you really do not belong? Does the "air" feel normal to you or does it leave you wanting fresh air? May the Lord grant that we continually run to Him for purification like no one and nothing else can provide.

FOR FURTHER STUDY

Sinclair B. Ferguson, *In Christ Alone: Living the Gospel Centered Life*

Martyn Lloyd-Jones, *The Assurance of Our Salvation (Studies in John 17): Exploring the Depth of Jesus' Prayer for His Own*

12

His Deepest Desires Revealed

MESSAGE INTRODUCTION

The room was silent as Jesus continued praying—probably as His disciples had never heard Him pray before. Judas had departed, and Peter likely sat disturbed about the denial Jesus had predicted. We saw in the last lesson that Jesus' prayer in John 17 corresponds to the high priest's ritual prayer on the Day of Atonement for himself, his family, and finally, his community. We see Jesus moving on from His petition for the Father to glorify His Son. In this lesson, we will consider Christ's ongoing prayer as He intercedes for the inner circle of disciples (verses 6 through 19) and finally for the entire church through the ages (verses 20 to 26). In the process, as Dr. Ferguson observes, we find Jesus revealing His "deepest desires" to His Father.

SCRIPTURE READINGS

John 17:6–26

LEARNING OBJECTIVES

1. To recognize the intercessory work of Jesus Christ in His prayers for His disciples
2. To appreciate the love of Christ for His inner circle of disciples
3. To connect Christ's longing for glory to the benefit He seeks for His followers

QUOTATION

Jesus Christ intercedes not only for great and eminent believers, but for the meanest and weakest; not for those only that are to be employed in the highest post of trust and honor in his kingdom, but for all, even those that in the eye of the world are inconsiderable. As the divine providence extends itself to the meanest creature, so does the divine grace to the meanest Christian. The good Shepherd has an eye even to the poor of the flock.

—Matthew Henry

LECTURE OUTLINE

A. Jesus prays for His inner circle of disciples.
　1. Jesus gives a detailed description of the disciples.
　　a. Those to whom Jesus has revealed the Father (John 17:6)
　　b. Those who have believed Jesus' Word and Jesus Himself (John 17:7)
　　c. Those whom Jesus has protected (John 17:12)
　　d. A description more complicated than the petition, revealing His love for them
　2. Jesus offers up a simple prayer for the disciples.
　　a. That, in summary, the Father would keep them
　　b. That the Father would keep them from the evil one while in this world (John 17:11, 15)
　　c. That the Father would sanctify them in the truth (John 17:17)
　　d. That they would be reserved ultimately for Jesus

B. Jesus prays for us as His disciples (John 17:20–26).
　1. He describes us as those "whom you have given me" (John 17:24).
　2. He prays for our unity (John 17:21).
　　a. Not organizational unity of the church as an institution
　　b. For the spiritual unity and fellowship of believers
　　c. Related to our love for one another in relation to Christ and for the impact of the world (John 17:23–26)
　3. He prays for us to be with Christ to see His glory (John 17:24).
　　a. With a "desire" that will not be expressed in the garden when He asks, "if you are willing," take this cup of suffering away (Luke 22:42)
　　b. With what He wants most, His glory, involving us

STUDY QUESTIONS

　1. While Jesus prayed, the disciples likely sat to the side discussing His petitions.
　　a. True
　　b. False

　2. As Jesus prayed, we find Him revealing some of His deepest desires.
　　a. True
　　b. False

　3. Jesus prayed for His inner circle of disciples in a manner similar to the high priest's praying for his family.
　　a. True
　　b. False

4. As Jesus prayed for His inner circle of followers, He gave a _____ description of them.
   a. Precise
   b. Vague
   c. Simple
   d. Detailed

5. As Jesus prayed for His inner circle of followers, He offered up a _____ petition for them.
   a. Precise
   b. Vague
   c. Simple
   d. Detailed

6. Regarding Jesus' description of His inner circle of disciples, He speaks of them as:
   a. Those to whom He has taught
   b. Those who have believed His Word
   c. Those whom He has protected
   d. Both a and b
   e. Both b and c

7. Regarding Jesus' petition for His inner circle of disciples, He offers up the prayer that:
   a. They would not mourn as the world does
   b. They would preach with boldness
   c. The Father would keep them from the evil one
   d. Both a and b
   e. All of the above

8. Regarding Jesus' prayer for us as His disciples:
   a. He describes us as those whom the Father has given him
   b. He prays for us to be with Him in glory
   c. He prays for the organizational/institutional unity of the church
   d. Both a and b
   e. All of the above

BIBLE STUDY

1. What is the difference between Jesus' "desire" for us as His disciples to be with Him (and so His petition, "Glorify your Son") and His more tentative "if you are willing" to take the cup away in the garden of Gethsemane (Luke 22:42)?

2. Examine Hebrews 7:25. How is the intercession mentioned in this verse alike and different from the intercession we read about in John 17?

3. Examine Psalm 2:8 in light of the entire psalm. How is this promise concretely fulfilled in John 17?

DISCUSSION QUESTIONS

1. What is the difference and likeness between the Lord's prayer here and the one that Jesus taught His disciples?

2. Dr. Ferguson calls attention to the 1987 Wimbledon tennis championship when Pat Cash of Australia defeated Ivan Lendl of Czechoslovakia. Upon his victory, rather than posing for protocol pictures with his trophy and receiving royal congratulations, Cash clambered into the crowd to hug his coach, family, and friends. Why did he do this, and how is this connected to Jesus' petition for His inner circle of disciples?

3. Consider the distinction that Dr. Ferguson makes between institutional and spiritual unity in relation to Christ's desire that Christians be "one." What is he getting at with this distinction, and what does it say about our cooperation with others in common causes?

APPLICATION

1. Did you ever stop to consider that Jesus has prayed for you if you are a Christian? Beyond that, did you ever reflect upon the fact that His current intercession in heaven means He continues to pray for you? How should this affect your relationship with and life before Him?

2. Dr. Ferguson speaks of Jesus' "favorite way" of regarding you as a love gift from the Father. We often speak of the gift of salvation (Rom. 6:23) that is so beneficial to the Christian life. How would it be beneficial to speak just as often about the fact that Christians are gifts received by the Savior?

3. It is fitting to use the final statement of Dr. Ferguson for a final matter of application: "We said at the beginning of these studies that it's so important for Jesus to stand at the center, and at the end of these studies, we feel we want him not only to be at the center, but we want him to be our all in all. And He has prayed that it will be true for you, because His Father gave you to Him before the foundation of the world in his love for Him and for you. What a Savior indeed!" Let these words soak in. As Jesus prayed (and continues to pray) that these desires would be true, why don't you as well, right now?

FOR FURTHER STUDY

Sinclair B. Ferguson, *In Christ Alone: Living the Gospel Centered Life*

Martyn Lloyd-Jones, *The Assurance of Our Salvation (Studies in John 17): Exploring the Depth of Jesus' Prayer for His Own*

George Newton, *An Exposition of John 17*